Alberto Ginastera

Danzas argentinas

opus 2

for piano • pour piano

with an introduction by
avec introduction de

Gérald Hugon

DURAND Editions Musicales

BOOSEY & HAWKES

edition dated 19 October 2016
édition du 19 octobre 2016

DF 16336

Durand Éditions ISMN : 9790044093540
Boosey & Hawkes ISMN: 9790051246892

Table of Contents – Table des matières

Danzas argentinas: echoes of rural Argentina

In Buenos Aires, during an official visit in September 1941, Aaron Copland had the opportunity to meet the young Ginastera. He wrote in his journal:

> There is a young composer here who is generally looked upon as the "white hope" of Argentine music. [...]. He is looked upon with favor by all groups here, is presentable, modest almost to a timid degree, and will, no doubt, someday be an outstanding figure in Argentine music.[1]

Ginastera was only 25 years old. He was born in Buenos Aires on 11 April 1916 to parents of Italian and Catalan origin. Already the composer of a ballet inspired by a legend of the Guaraní Indians, *Panambí*, Opus 1 (1935–37), and of pieces for piano influenced by Argentinian popular music, such as *Danzas argentinas*, Opus 2, the *Tres piezas*, Opus 6 (1937–40) and *Malambo*, Opus 7 (1940), at that time he was composing his second ballet, *Estancia*, Opus 8, based on the rural life of Argentina.

In 1967, he reflected that his works could be divided into three periods which he described retrospectively as "objective nationalism" (1935–48), "subjective nationalism" (1948–57), and "neo-expressionism" (from 1958). Gilbert Chase explained that:

> Ginastera's objective nationalism is characterized by the presentation of Argentine traits and themes in a direct, overt manner, with tonal melodic elements. Both rhythm and melody are modelled on types of Argentine folksong and dance known as *música criolla* (of European provenance), though literal quotations are seldom used.[2]

Date of composition: 1937
First performance: Buenos Aires, 27 October 1937, by Antonio de Raco
Dedications:
  No 1: Pedro A Sáenz[3]
  No 2: Emilia L Stahlberg[4]
  No 3: Antonio de Raco[5]
Manuscript: presumed lost
Published: Durand, Paris, 1939, D&F 13004

The *Danzas argentinas* belong to the period of "objective nationalism". Ginastera composed the work while he was still a student at the Conservatorio Nacional of Buenos Aires, at the same time as he was finishing his first ballet, *Panambí*, Opus 1.

In his article "Homage to Béla Bartók"[6] he remarked:

> When I composed my *Danzas argentinas* for piano in 1937, Bartók's influence was present. My "imaginary folklore" begins there, with polytonal harmonisation, its strong, marked rhythms—the Bartókian "feverish excitement"—all within a total pianism where the spirit of a national music is recreated.

The pianist Barbara Nissman, dedicatee of Ginastera's last composition, the *Third Piano Sonata*, Opus 55 (1982), attested:

> Ginastera had an instinctive knowledge of the keyboard—an uncanny ability to exploit a wide range of its coloristic and rhythmic possibilities, its lyrical and percussive qualities. And yet he always knew what was innately "pianistic"—what would work and fit comfortably under the hand.[7]

This collection consists of three dances in §, organised by tempi: fast – slow – fast. The brevity of the elements used indicates their popular origin.

---

[1] Quoted from Simon Wright, *Panambí / Estancia*, sleeve note, Conifer Classics, 75605 51336 2, p 13.

[2] Gilbert Chase, "Alberto Ginastera", *The New Grove Dictionary of Music and Musicians*, London, Macmillan Publishers Limited, 1980, edited by Stanley Sadie, vol 7, p 388.

[3] Pedro Sáenz (1915–95), Argentinian composer. He was, like Ginastera, a student at the Conservatorio Williams and at the Conservatorio Nacional de Música in Buenos Aires (1936–39).

[4] No biographical details of this dedicatee have been found.

[5] Antonio de Raco (1915–2010), Argentine pianist.

[6] Alberto Ginastera, "Homage to Béla Bartók", *Tempo*, n° 136, March, 1981, p 4.

[7] Barbara Nissman, "Remembering Alberto Ginastera", *Piano Today,* 1 July 2007, http://www.barbaranissman. com/#!remembering-ginastera/c1vnh.

From this work of his youth, Ginastera would have been able to affirm that which he stated at the end of his life:

> To compose, in my opinion, is to create an architecture, to formulate an order and set in values certain structures ... In music, this architecture unfolds in time.[8]

---

[8] Simon Wright, op cit, p 13.

Leaving aside the study of the popular sources that would be very interesting and completely justified in the present case, we have preferred, from a more universal perspective, to focus in an analytic way on the general structure of these pieces, with the aim of enabling performers to understand them more quickly and respond better to their musical substance.

I. Danza del viejo boyero (Dance of the old herdsman)

This piece is conceived entirely in a bitonal fashion. Earlier examples of bitonality, from the start of the 20th century, include Bartók's first *Bagatelle* (1908) and the third piece of *Sarcasms* by Prokofiev (1914).

The principle maintained here—white keys played by the right hand, black by the left—has the following melodic and harmonic consequences:

1) the right hand plays in Phrygian mode (white notes E to E), or in Ionian mode (white notes C to C, or C Major)

2) the left hand plays two forms of a diatonic pentatonic mode:[9] the first (p_1) G♭–A♭– B♭–D♭–E♭ and the fifth (p_5) E♭–G♭–A♭–B♭–D♭.

Notice in the right hand a unifying chord (**h**) of a second and a third in two forms (major second/minor third or minor second/major third)

which affects the general colour in a prominent way.

The rhythmic writing, with its perpetual motion of quavers in ⅜ bears a similarity to the *malambo*, a rapid, energetic dance characteristic of *gaucho* culture.[10]

The formal construction, in two unequal parts, is organised around a climax at the mid-point (bars 34–45), set about a pause.

The theme (**A**) in bars 1–8 is reiterated twice, like a refrain, in bars 40–48 and 62–70.

---

[9] Vincent Persichetti, *Twentieth-Century Harmony. Creative Aspects and Practice*, WW Norton & Company, New York • London, 1961, p 51.

[10] See also Ginastera's *Malambo* Opus 7 for piano, Ricordi Americana SAEC, Buenos Aires, 1947, BA 8449.

Two planes of sonority, sounded alternately by the two hands, form a single musical line. The left hand evokes the guitar, while in the right hand the upper note of each chord should be controlled to intensify the minimalist melodic design that has the feel of popular music. It is good to draw attention, right from the first reading, to the presence of an intentional, gentle irregularity—the B♭ added in bars 2, 42 and 64 to the first beat in the left hand.

Notice the dynamic levels in each of the three occurrences: *p/più p, mf/p, pp/più pp*.

The second theme (**B**) is stated three times in a dynamic progression *p/mf/f*.

It consists of four fragments of two bars, following the pattern **b-b'-b-b''**—in which **b'** (bars 13–14) differs from **b** only in the descending third at the end. **b''** introduces a new rhythm.

In the left hand there is a rhythmic ostinato of six notes in a bar, limited to four pitches.

At the first appearance, B_1 (bars 11–18), the left hand plays in mode p_5; in the second, B_2 (bars 19–25), the left hand plays in mode p_1 while the right hand plays the theme, transposed up a fourth. The third appearance, B_3 (bars 27–34), is a reproduction of **B1**, but transposed up an octave with the addition of extra right-hand quavers (eighth notes) in bars 27, 29 and 31.

To move between these statements of the theme, Ginastera uses links: in bars 8–10 (the start of theme **A** and chord **h**); and in bar 26 (right hand chords **h**, left hand mode ascending p_1).

The climax at the halfway point (bars 34–40) is achieved by two phrases, rhythmically derived from **b''**. The first of these (bars 34–36) omits the lower fourth of chord **h** as well as the ostinato in the left hand, which here plays in rhythmic unison with the right. The second phrase (bars 36–40) abandons bitonality in favour of "white-note" chords.

After a restatement of the theme **A** (bars 40–48) and a transition in bars 48–52 (mode p_5), a new rhythmic and melodic version of the second theme (B_4) appears in bars 52–61. This is two octaves higher than B_2, with a fourth dynamic, *pp*, not previously used for this theme. Instead of the ostinato, the left hand plays in rhythmic unison with the right. The increased note values in bars 58–61 contribute to the *ritenuto*.

A final return to theme **A** (bars 62–70) precedes the coda (bars 70–81), which begins with the two elements of the initial theme and rises bit by bit until it disappears. There follows a spread chord E_2–A_2–D_3–G_3–B_3–E_4,[11] the six open strings of the guitar, an instrument so typical of Argentine popular music. Then, in a low register, a chromatic motif played *mf*, and a very low E, tonic of the Phrygian mode.

---

[11] This chord contains the five notes of the pentatonic scale: E, G, A, B, D.

II. Danza de la moza donosa (Dance of the pretty girl)

Of the pieces in the set, this one is closest to popular song. The two phrases of the initial melody reflect respectively the eight- and five-syllable articulations of popular poetry.

It is in a three-part form: **A** (bars 1–24)—**B** (bars 25–60)—**A'** (bars 59–81), with a slight overlap at the return of **A'**.

A short introduction (bars 1–3) establishes a *zamba* rhythm (three quavers, quaver, crotchet; or three eighth notes, eighth note, quarter note)

which is constant throughout the piece (apart from bars 40, 46, 48, 50, 54 and 80–81).

Part **A** (bars 4–24) consists of two sections:

1) Two expressive phrases each of four bars: **a** (bars 4–7) & **a'** (bars 8–11), which differ only in the way they finish. Each one is divided into two contrasting two-bar motifs.

2) Three four-bar phrases a_1 (bars 12–15), a_2 (bars 16–19), a_3 (bars 20–24), derived rhythmically and melodically from the first section. The first two have chromatic countermelodies.

The central part, **B**, also consists of two sections:[12]

1) two eight-bar phrases in dynamic progression, b_1 (bars 25–32) and b_2 (bars 33–40), then:

2) two intense phrases written in a more specifically pianistic fashion.

The first phrase, b_3, consists of eight bars divided into two four-bar groups:

• in the first group (bars 41–44), the right-hand chord shape is two perfect fourths separated by a major second;

• in the second (bars 45–48), the chord shape is an augmented fourth and a perfect fourth separated by a minor second.

The second phrase, b_4, similarly in two groups, marks the climax of the piece, *ff* (bars 49–52, in which the right hand of bars 41–44 is transposed an octave higher), before the quietening, slightly extended second group (bars 53–60), which leads to the return of the opening material.

Throughout part **B**, the left hand maintains the rhythmic ostinato of **A**, but in a wide variety of melodic and harmonic configurations, always rising (apart from bars 46, 48, 50 and 54).

After a restatement of the introduction (bars 59–61), the return of the two parts of section **A** is modified as follows:

1) **a-a'** adds a lower third, like the harmonization of a popular song

2) a_3 repeated twice (bars 70–73 and 74–77), slightly altered: in bars 70 and 74 a lower third is added, followed in each case by a three-bar dotted-minim (half-note) counter-melody a sixth lower, with an extension in bars 78–79.

In the *codetta*, rising fifths (A–E) ascend to a final dissonant chord consisting of the minor sixth, major sixth and raised third (C♯) of A minor.

---

[12] Each phrase or part-phrase mentioned here includes the upbeat of the previous bar.

III. Danza del gaucho matrero (Dance of the cunning gaucho)

Before 1850, the *gauchos* were free, nomadic people who lived in the pampas, until the introduction of barbed wire fencing to enclose the *estancias* (large privately-owned estates) reduced their freedom of movement. In order to survive and avoid being marginalised, they often had to remain fixed in one place as salaried labourers.

This piece, made up of three principal ideas, falls neatly into two parts because of the way these ideas are reiterated and modified. The three themes are linked by transitional elements.

General form

Formal function	Bars	Contents by section
Part I	1–155	
Theme A	1–16	2 phrases (8+8)
Transition I	17–32	3 segments (4+4+8)
Theme A	33–48	Verbatim repetition (apart from right-hand chords, bars 39–40 & 47–48)
Transition I'	49–57	Segment I only with extension
Theme B	58–70	4 statements
Transition II	71–102	Fourth-chord motif **z** (predominantly rhythmic)
Theme C	103–155	Three-part structure, C Major, A minor, C Major: four-bar element **c** and its variants
Part II	156–223	
Theme A	156–171	Restatement with chords (y_3/y_4) & (y_2/y_6)
Transition I'	172–181	Repetition, only varied by the addition of octaves *sf* in the right hand (bars 174 & 176)
Theme B	182–194	Variation: perfect chords in the right hand replaced by octaves
Transition II	195–210	Limited to fourth-chord motif **z** and its variants
Theme C	211–223	Shortened modules **c** (twice) & c_1 (twice)
Coda	224–232	224–227 Repetitive extensions / glissandos / conclusion in C Major

Some observations about each of these elements:

Theme A
Structure of the phrase (bars 1–8)

The germ motif consists of six quavers in rhythmic

unison, in contrary motion: descending major thirds in the right hand, ascending fifths in the left.

This is built into four-bar phrases: in each of these, the germ motif is repeated three times, each with different endings:

  ▪ bars 3–4: left hand, Locrian[13] mode descending; right hand, six-note motif transposed

  ▪ bars 7–8: left hand, Locrian mode descending; right hand, two chords **y** (y_1/y_2) (perfect fourth and major third separated by a minor second).

When the phrase is repeated in bars 15–16, two more transpositions of chord **y** (y_3/y_4) appear:

---

[13] In terms of intervals, B to B on the white keys—but here transposed to C.

Chords **y**:

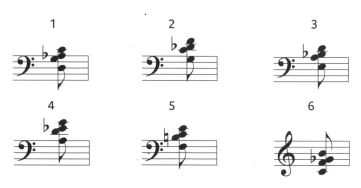

Transition I

This first transition appears in three segments according to the following types of voicing:

1) Bars 17–20: left-hand ostinato alternating major and minor seconds; right hand in minor seconds.

2) Bars 21–24: left-hand uninterrupted texture on the black-keys, alternating fifths and fourths in groups of four quavers; right-hand chords (y_3/y_5). Note the augmented fourth in variant y_5.

3) Bars 25–32: left-hand ostinato; right-hand chord y_2.

A sort of **fragmentary reprise** follows, made up of the preceding elements: bars 33–48 repetition of theme **A** with tiny differences, bars 39–40 chords (y_3/y_4), bars 47–48 chords (y_2/y_6), followed by the first section of Transition I, with interruptions in the left-hand ostinato (bars 51 and 53), and a rhythmically accelerating extension which culminates in bar 57 with a right-hand glissando.

Theme B

More diatonic than theme **A**, this melody has a popular character with the right hand in major triads.

There are four statements. The first two (bars 58–61 and 61–64) are strictly identical; the last two (bars 64–67 and 67–70) are like an ascending development of the preceding ones with a variant on the final chords played at the upper octave. The rhythm contains hemiola[14] (60, 63, 66, 69).

---

[14] Rhythmic effect characteristic of *música criolla*, achieved by the use of notes in duple divisions (crotchets, for example) in compound bars where the beats are divisible into three (for example dotted crotchets in §).

Transition II in two segments

More complex than Transition I, this contains in its two segments the germs of development:

1) Bars 71–82: this section is once again bitonal. The left hand plays on the black keys in pentatonic mode, first in fifths (except at bars 74–75, in scales descending by tones), then in fourths (bars 80–82).

In the right hand, the motif **z** appearing at bars 72–73 in fourth chords will later occur in different variants at bars 195–210.

2) Bars 83–102: the bitonality gives way to a more unstable section, in four stages as follows:

▪ IIa bars 83–85: continuation of bars 80–82, the phrase ending with rhythm **z**.

▪ IIb bars 86–89: melodic variant of the rhythm of **z**, alternating twice with bar 17.

▪ IIc bars 90–92: melodic variant of the rhythm of **z**, transposed twice.

▪ IId bars 93–102: bitonal stabilisation (left hand E Major, right hand E-flat Major), alternating perfect and augmented chords.

Theme C

Marked "violente", this theme presents the brutal character of *malambo*.

Basically diatonic, it is focused on the low register of the instrument, in the key of C Major, and has a middle section in A-flat Major (bars 121–132).

The four-bar element **c** (bars 105–108) is repeated in bars 109–112. In bars 108 and 112, notice the chords in hemiola.

This element represents a rhythmic structure from which various figures are derived:

▪ **c'** (bars 113–116): a variant of **c** with hemiola ending at bar 116

▪ c_1 (bars 117–118): a combination drawn from bars 113 and 116 respectively, and repeated in bars 119–120.

In the central part in A-flat Major, the left hand plays four arpeggiated flat notes.

The right hand plays c_2 (derived from c_1) in bars 121–122, repeated three times in bars 127–132, and c'' (bars 123–126), which has the same rhythmic identity as c but a different harmonic configuration.

In the right hand, the repetition links c_1 (133–134), c twice (135–142), then c_1 twice (143–146).

At the conclusion (bars 147–155) the motif seems to restate c_1 (bar 147), but the harmonies fade, *diminuendo*, to an ostinato of two bars of quavers (eighth notes).

Gérald Hugon
(translation by Anthony Marks)

Danzas argentinas: échos de l'Argentine rurale

À Buenos Aires, lors d'un voyage officiel en septembre 1941, Aaron Copland eut l'opportunité de rencontrer le jeune Ginastera. Il nota dans son journal :

> Il y a ici un jeune compositeur qui est généralement considéré comme « le grand espoir » de la musique argentine. [...] Il est regardé ici de façon favorable par tous, il est correct, modeste, presque timide même et il deviendra, sans aucun doute, un jour, une figure exceptionnelle de la musique argentine[1].

Ginastera n'avait que vingt-cinq ans. Il était né à Buenos Aires le 11 avril 1916 de parents d'origine italienne et catalane. Déjà l'auteur d'un ballet inspiré d'une légende des indiens Guaranís, *Panambí* (1935–1937), de pièces pour piano telles les *Danzas argentinas* opus 2, les *Tres Piezas* opus 6 (1937–1940), ou le *Malambo* opus 7 (1940) influencées par les musiques populaires de l'Argentine, il composait alors son second ballet, *Estancia* opus 8, basé sur la vie rurale argentine.

En 1967, il considérait que son œuvre pouvait être divisée en trois périodes qu'il qualifiait respectivement de «nationalisme objectif» (1935–1947), de «nationalisme subjectif» (1948–1957) et de «néo-expressionnisme» à partir de 1958.

Gilbert Chase expliquait :

> Le nationalisme objectif de Ginastera est caractérisé par une présentation des expressions et sujets argentins, d'une manière directe et manifeste, avec des éléments mélodiques attachés à la tonalité. À la fois le rythme et la mélodie sont modelés sur des genres argentins du chant populaire et de danse connus sous le nom de *música criolla* (d'origine européenne), bien que les citations littérales soient rarement employées[2].

Date de composition : 1937
Première audition: Buenos Aires, 27 octobre 1937, Antonio de Raco
Dédicaces:
  nº 1 Pedro A Sáenz[3]
  nº 2 Emilia L Stahlberg[4]
  nº 3 Antonio de Raco[5]
Manuscrit : présumé perdu
Édition : Durand, Paris, 1939, D&F 13004

Les *Danzas argentinas* appartiennent à la période du «nationalisme objectif». Ginastera composa l'œuvre alors qu'il était encore étudiant au Conservatorio Nacional de Buenos Aires, en même temps qu'il achevait son premier ballet, *Panambí* opus 1.

Dans son article « Homage to Béla Bartók »[6] il fit remarquer :

> Quand je composais mes *Danzas argentinas* pour piano en 1937, l'influence de Bartók était présente. Mon «folklore imaginaire» commence là, avec l'harmonisation polytonale, avec ses rythmes puissants et marqués—la «surexcitation fiévreuse bartokienne»—tout cela dans une écriture pianistique où l'esprit de la musique nationale est recréé.

La pianiste Barbara Nissman, dédicataire de la *Troisième Sonate* pour piano opus 55 (1982), ultime composition de Ginastera, témoigne :

> Ginastera avait une connaissance instinctive du clavier, une capacité audacieuse d'exploiter une grande étendue de ses possibilités de couleurs et de rythmes, de ses qualités lyriques et percussives. Et cependant, il savait toujours ce qui était foncièrement «pianistique», ce qui fonctionnerait et tomberait confortablement sous la main[7].

---

[1] Cité d'après Simon Wright, *Panambí / Estancia*, sleeve note, Conifer Classics, 75605 51336 2, p 21.

[2] Gilbert Chase, «Alberto Ginastera», *The New Grove Dictionary of Music and Musicians*, London, Macmillan Publishers Limited, 1980, edited by Stanley Sadie, vol 7, p 388.

[3] Pedro Sáenz (1915–1995), compositeur argentin. Il fut comme Ginastera étudiant au Conservatoire Williams ainsi qu'au Conservatorio Nacional de Buenos Aires (1936–1939).

[4] Aucune information biographique a été retrouvée.

[5] Antonio de Raco (1915–2010), pianiste argentin.

[6] Alberto Ginastera, «Homage to Béla Bartók», *Tempo*, nº 136, mars 1981, p 4.

[7] Barbara Nissman, «Remembering Alberto Ginastera», *Piano Today,* 1er juillet 2007, http://www.barbaranissman.com/#!remembering-ginastera/c1vnh.

Ce recueil comprend trois danses en 𝄋 organisées quant aux tempi selon le schéma vif–lent–vif. La brièveté des éléments mis en œuvre indique l'origine populaire des matériaux.

Dès cette œuvre de jeunesse, Ginastera aurait déjà pu affirmer ce qu'il déclara à la fin de sa vie : « Composer, selon moi, c'est créer une architecture, formuler un ordre et mettre en valeurs certaines structures... En musique, cette architecture se développe dans le temps »[8].

Écartant l'étude des sources populaires qui serait tout à fait intéressante et justifiée dans le cas présent, nous avons préféré, dans une perspective plus universelle, souligner de manière analytique les structures générales de ces pièces, afin de permettre aux interprètes de les appréhender plus rapidement et de mieux s'en approprier la substance musicale.

---

[8] Simon Wright, op cit, p 22.

I. Danza del viejo boyero (Danse du vieux vacher)

Ce morceau est entièrement conçu de manière bitonale. On avait déjà encontré des exemples de bitonalité, dès les premières années du XXᵉ siècle comme dans la *Bagatelle nº 1* (1908) de Bartók et la troisième pièce des *Sarcasmes* (1914) de Prokofiev.

Le principe retenu ici, touches blanches jouées par la main droite (md) et touches noires jouées par la main gauche (mg), a pour conséquences mélodiques et harmoniques que :

1) la md joue en mode de *mi* (phrygien) ou en mode de *do* (ionien ou tonalité d'*ut* majeur)

2) la mg joue deux formes du mode pentatonique diatonique[9] : la première (p_1) *sol♭–la♭–si♭–ré♭–mi♭* et la cinquième (p_5) *mi♭–sol♭–la♭–si♭–ré♭*.

On remarquera à la md un accord unificateur **(h)** seconde/tierce sous deux formes (seconde majeure/tierce mineure ou seconde mineure/tierce majeure)

qui conditionne, de manière prédominante, la couleur générale.

L'écriture rythmique avec son mouvement perpétuel de croches dans une mesure à 𝄋 s'apparente au *malambo*, une danse virile rapide et énergique, caractéristique de la culture *gaucho*[10].

La construction formelle en deux parties non équivalentes est organisée autour d'un climax médian (mes 34–40) figé sur un point d'orgue.

---

[9] Vincent Persichetti, *Twentieth-Century Harmony Creative Aspects and Practice*, WW Norton & Company, New York • London, 1961, p 51.

[10] Voir aussi le *Malambo* opus 7 pour piano de Ginastera, Ricordi Americana SAEC, Buenos Aires, 1947, BA 8449.

Le thème (**A**) (mes 1–8) est réitéré deux fois à la manière d'un refrain (40–48 & 62–70).

Deux plans sonores répartis en alternance aux deux mains forment une seule ligne. La mg évoque la guitare tandis qu'à la md, la note supérieure de chaque accord doit être contrôlée pour renforcer le dessin mélodique minimaliste de caractère populaire. Il est bon de porter attention, dès la première lecture, à la présence d'une légère irrégularité intentionnelle, le *si♭* mg ajouté aux premiers temps mes 2/42/64.

On remarquera les niveaux dynamiques de chacune des trois occurrences : *p* / *più p*, *mf* / *p*, *pp* / *più pp*.

Le second thème (**B**) est exposé trois fois dans une progression dynamique *p* / *mf* / *f*.

Il est constitué de quatre fragments de deux mesures selon le schéma **b b' b b''** dans lequel **b'** (mes 13–14) diffère de **b** seulement dans sa désinence descendante en tierces. **b''** introduit un nouveau rythme.

À la mg s'installe un ostinato rythmique de six notes par mesure, limité à quatre hauteurs.

Le premier exposé **B₁** (mes 11–18), la mg joue dans le mode (p_5) ; dans le second **B₂** (mes 19–25) la mg joue dans le mode ($\mathbf{p_1}$), tandis que la md joue le thème, transposé à la quarte supérieure. Le troisième exposé $\mathbf{B_3}$ (mes 27–34) est la reproduction de $\mathbf{B_1}$ mais à l'octave supérieure avec, à la md, l'ajout de croches aux mes 27, 29 et 31.

Pour assurer les transitions, Ginastera utilise des liens mes 8–10 (tête de (**A**) + accord (**h**)), et mes 26 (md accords (**h**), mg mode ascendant ($\mathbf{p_1}$)).

Le climax médian (mes 34–40) s'effectue avec deux phrases, dont le rythme est issu de **b''**. La première (mes 34–36) élimine la quarte inférieure de l'accord (**h**) ainsi que l'ostinato de la mg, qui joue alors en rythme parallèle avec la md. La seconde (mes 36–40) abandonne la bitonalité. Les sons des accords appartiennent aux touches blanches.

Après un retour de **A** (mes 40–48) et une transition mes 48–52 (mode ($\mathbf{p_5}$)), survient une nouvelle variation rythmique et mélodique du second thème $\mathbf{B_4}$ (mes 52–61) transposé dans l'aigu à deux octaves

de $\mathbf{B_2}$, dans une quatrième dynamique pp, non encore utilisée pour ce thème. En remplacement de l'ostinato à la mg, se trouve une ligne homorythmique avec la md. L'augmentation des valeurs des durées aux mes 58–61 participe au ***ritenuto***.

Un dernier retour au thème **A** (mes 62–70) précède la coda (mes 70–81) qui commence avec les deux éléments du thème initial et s'élève peu à peu jusqu'à extinction. Se succèdent un accord égrené, l'accord $mi_2 - la_2 - ré_3 - sol_3 - si_3 - mi_4$,[11] des six cordes à vide de la guitare, l'instrument typique de la musique populaire argentine, puis dans le registre grave, un motif chromatique joué mf et un mi à l'extrême grave, tonique du mode phrygien.

_____

[11] Cet accord comporte les cinq sons du mode pentatonique sur mi–sol–la–si–$ré$.

II. Danza de la moza donosa (Danse de la jolie paysanne)

Voici la pièce du recueil la plus proche du chant populaire. Le caractère chanté des deux phrases de la mélodie initiale reflète respectivement l'articulation octosyllabique et pentasyllabique d'une poésie populaire.

Il s'agit d'une forme tripartite **A** (mes 1–24)—**B** (mes 25–60)—**A'** (mes 59–81), avec un léger chevauchement au retour de **A'**.

Une courte introduction (mes 1–3) installe à la mg un rythme de *zamba* (trois croches – croche – noire)

constant dans tout le morceau, excepté aux mes 40, 46, 48, 50, 54 et 80–81.

La partie **A** (mes 4–24) comporte deux sections :

1) deux phrases expressives similaires de 4 mesures **a** (mes 4–7) & **a'** (mes 8–11), différenciées seulement par leur terminaison, chacune divisée en deux motifs contrastants de 2 mesures

2) trois phrases de quatre mesures $\mathbf{a_1}$ (mes 12–15), $\mathbf{a_2}$ (mes 16–19), $\mathbf{a_3}$ (mes 20–24), dérivées rythmiquement et mélodiquement de la première section, avec contre-chants chromatiques pour les deux premières.

La partie médiane **B** comporte aussi deux sections[12] :

1) deux phrases en progression dynamique de

huit mesures $\mathbf{b_1}$ (mes 25–32) et $\mathbf{b_2}$ (mes 33–40)

2) deux phrases intenses et d'une écriture plus spécifiquement pianistique.

La première $\mathbf{b_3}$ de huit mesures constituées de deux membres de quatre mesures :

■ (mes 41–44), md l'accord comporte deux quartes justes séparées par une seconde majeure.

■ (mes 45–48), md l'accord présente quarte augmentée et quarte juste séparées par seconde mineure.

La seconde $\mathbf{b_4}$ également en deux membres, marque d'abord le climax de la pièce ff (mes 49–52, md transposition à l'octave supérieure des mes 41–44), avant l'apaisement du second membre avec une extension (mes 53–60), conduisant au retour de la partie initiale.

Pendant toute cette seconde partie, la mg poursuit l'ostinato rythmique de **A**, mais dans une grande variété de configurations melodico-harmoniques, toujours ascendantes à l'exception des mesures 46, 48, 50 & 54.

Après la reprise de l'introduction (mes 59–61), le retour des deux sections de **A** est modifié ainsi :

1) **a-a'** ajout de tierce inférieure à la manière d'une harmonisation de chant populaire

2) reprise de $\mathbf{a_3}$ modifié par deux fois (70–73/74–77), puis tierce inférieure ajoutée (mes 70 et 74) et contre-chant en blanches pointées à la sixte inférieure à partir des mesures suivantes, avec extension de deux mesures (78–79).

La *codetta* présente des quintes ascendantes *la–mi* jusqu'à l'accord final dissonant avec sixte mineure et sixte majeure et la tierce picarde (*do* ♯) de *la* mineur.

_____

[12] Chaque phrase ou membre de phrase ici mentionnés comprend la levée de la mesure précédente au numéro du début indiqué.

III. Danza del gaucho matrero (Danse du gaucho malin)

Avant 1850, le *gaucho* était un personnage nomade et libre qui vivait dans la *pampa*. L'introduction du « fil de fer barbelé » vint à délimiter les « estancias » (grandes propriétés terriennes) et réduire sa liberté de circulation. Pour subsister et éviter la marginalité, le *gaucho* fut le plus souvent contraint de se fixer comme salarié sédentaire (*peón*).

Cette pièce, constituée de trois idées principales, s'articule nettement en deux parties en raison de la réexposition modifiée des trois éléments. Ces trois thèmes sont reliés par des éléments de transition.

Forme générale

Fonction formelle	Mesures	Contenus sectionnels
Partie I	1–155	
Thème A	1–16	2 phrases (8+8)
Transition I	17–32	3 segments (4+4+8)
Thème A	33–48	reprise littérale sauf accords md (39–40 & 47–48)
Transition I'	49–57	segment I seul avec extension
Thème B	58–70	4 exposés
Transition II	71–102	motif accord de quartes **z** prédominant rythmiquement
Thème C	103–155	structure tripartie *ut* majeur –*la* bémol –*ut* majeur module **c** et ses dérivés
Partie II	156–223	
Thème A	156–171	réexposition avec accords (y_3/y_4) & (y_2/y_6)
Transition I'	172–181	reprise seulement variée md (174 & 176) avec ajout d'octaves sf
Thème B	182–194	variation: remplacement des accords parfaits md par des octaves
Transition II	195–210	limitée au motif accord de quartes **z** et ses dérivés
Thème C	211–223	abrégé modules **c** (deux fois) & c_1 (deux fois)
Coda	224–232	224–227 extension répétitive / glissandi / conclusion en *ut* majeur

Quelques observations à propos de chacun de ces éléments :

Thème A
Structure de la phrase (mes 1–8)

Le motif générateur comprend six croches

présentées dans une écriture isorythmique en mouvements contraires: md tierces majeures descendantes / mg quintes ascendantes.

Chacun des membres de la phrase de quatre mesures est constitué du motif de six croches, trois fois répété avec terminaisons différentes :

- mes 3–4 mg mode locrien[13] descendant / md motif de six notes transposé;
- mes 7–8 mg mode locrien descendant / md deux accords **y** (y_1/y_2) (structure quarte juste et tierce majeure séparée par seconde mineure).

À la répétition de la phrase, mes 15–16, sont proposées deux nouvelles transpositions de l'accord **y** (y_3/y_4):

---

[13] Mode de *si* ici transposé sur *do*.

Accords **y**:

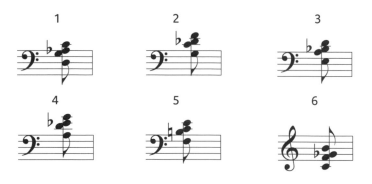

Transition I

Cette première transition se présente en trois segments selon les modes d'activité sonores suivants :

1) mes 17–20, mg ostinato de secondes majeure/mineure alternant ; md en secondes mineures

2) mes 21–24, mg continuum sonore sur les notes noires alternant quintes et quartes par groupes de quatre croches avec md accords (y_3/y_5). Remarquer la variante y_5 avec quarte augmentée

3) mes 25–32, mg ostinato de 12 croches avec md accord y_2.

Suit alors une sorte de **reprise fragmentaire** des éléments exposés jusqu'ici : mes 33–48 répétition du thème **A** avec d'infimes différences, mes 39 & 40 accords (y_3/y_4) et mes 47–48 accords (y_2/y_6) suivi par le segment I de la Transition I, avec rupture de l'ostinato de secondes, mg (mes 51 & 53) et par une extension en accélération rythmique aboutissant mes 57 à un glissando de la md.

Thème B

Plus diatonique que **A**, c'est une mélodie de caractère populaire avec md en accords parfaits.

Il y a quatre exposés, les deux premiers, strictement identiques (mes 58–61 & mes 61–64), les deux derniers comme une métamorphose ascendante des précédents (mes 64–67 & mes 67–70) avec une variante aux deux derniers accords joués à l'octave supérieure.

Le rythme comporte des hémioles[14] (60, 63, 66, 69).

---

[14] Effet rythmique caractéristique de la *música criolla* engendré par l'emploi de notes de division binaire (par ex noire) dans une mesure ternaire où l'unité de temps, (par ex la noire pointée en §), est divisible en trois.

Transition II en deux segments

Plus complexe que la première transition, elle présente dans ses deux segments des tendances au développement :

1) mes 71–82 : il s'agit d'une section à nouveau bitonale. La mg joue sur les notes noires en mode pentatonique d'abord en quintes (excepté aux mes 74–75, en gamme par tons descendante) puis en quartes (mes 80–82).

À la md le motif **z** présenté aux mes 72–73 en accords de quartes, connaîtra différentes variantes mes 195–210.

2) Mes 83–102, l'abandon de la bitonalité ouvre sur un segment encore plus instable en quatre paliers ainsi caractérisés :

▪ IIa mes 83–85, continuation des mes 80–82 avec terminaison sur le rythme de **z**

▪ IIb mes 86–89, variante mélodique sur rythme de **z** alternant deux fois avec la mes 17

▪ IIc mes 90–92, variante mélodique sur rythme de **z** transposée deux fois

▪ IId mes 93–102, stabilisation bitonale (mg *mi* majeur/md *mi* bémol majeur) alternant accords parfaits et accords augmentés.

Thème C

Marqué « violente », ce thème présente le caractère brutal du *malambo*.

Foncièrement diatonique, il est concentré dans le registre grave de l'instrument, dans la tonalité de *do* majeur et comporte une partie médiane en *la* bémol majeur (121–132).

Le module **c** de quatre mesures (mes 105–108) est répété mesures 109–112. On observe à la md aux mesures 108 & 112, les accords en hémiole :

Ce module constitue la structure rythmique d'où seront dérivées différentes figures :

▪ **c'** (mes 113–116) variante de **c** avec l'hémiole abandonnée mes 116.

▪ **c_1** (mes 117–118) combinaison provenant respectivement des mes 113 & 116 répétées mes 119–120.

Dans la partie médiane en *la* bémol majeur, la mg est arpégée sur quatre notes bémolisées.

La md joue c_2 (dérivé de c_1) mes 121–122, trois fois répété (mes 127–132) et c'' (mes 123–126) par identité rythmique avec c, mais dans une configuration harmonique différente.

À la md, la reprise enchaîne c_1 (133–134), deux fois c (135–142) puis deux fois c_1 (143–146).

La conclusion mes 147–155 le motif semble reprendre c_1 mes 147, mais les harmonies s'effacent *diminuendo* sur un ostinato de deux mesures en croches.

Gérald Hugon

DANZAS ARGENTINAS
opus 2
for piano • pour piano

Alberto Ginastera

a Pedro A Sáenz

I. Danza del viejo boyero

Animato ed allegro (♩. = 138)

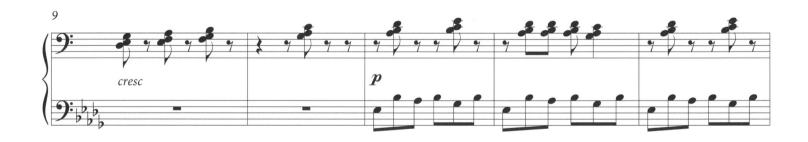

a Emilia L Stahlberg

II. Danza de la moza donosa

a Antonio de Raco

III. Danza del gaucho matrero

Buenos Aires, 1937